Bring Joy to Vietnam

A Journal of Notes

By

Joy Wilkerson

ISBN: 1-4107-4006-4(e-book)
ISBN: 1-4107-4005-6(Paperback)

Librrary of Congress Control Number: 2003092386

This book is printed on acid free paper.

Printed in the United States of America
Bloomington, IN

1st Books - rev. 04/21/03

DEDICATION:

I dedicate my book to all the Vietnam Veterans.

I also give special thanks to Dale Robertson and members of the press for

making my journey to see my pen pals in Vietnam possible.

Thank you

Joy Wilkerson

Table of Contents:

BRING JOY TO VIETNAM, OR HAVE CAPITAL, COMPASSION AND A TYPEWRITER, WILL TRAVEL

MY DEAR FRIEND, MR SAM BERNS OF THE USO, HAD BEEN AFTER ME TO WRITE DOWN ALL THAT I COULD REMEMBER ABOUT HOW THE "BRING JOY TO VIETNAM CAMPAIGN" BEGAN, AND, BELIEVE ME, IT IS RATHER A LENGTHY, INVOLVED, HARDWORKING, RED-EYED, SWOLLEN KNUCKLED, BROKE, TIRED, LEG-CRAMPED, HEADACHY, TENSE, DEPRESSING, WONDERFUL EXPERIENCE THAT I HAVE TO RELATE.

THERE WAS NO BETTER WAY TO MEET AS MANY OF MY LOYAL, DEVOTED, UP-IN-THE-CLOUDS, DOWN-IN–THE-DUMPS, FUNNY, SENSITIVE, LONELY, APPRECIATIVE, HARDWORKING, BRAVE, GROUP-PROUD FRIENDS OR, AS SHOWBIZ PEOPLE WOULD REFER TO THEM, FANS. TO ME, HOWEVER, WE ARE LIFETIME FRIENDS. BEING A FRIEND TO THE MEN OF THE MILITARY HAS CAUSED ME A FEW EMBARRASSING MOMENTS. SOME OF THE PEOPLE IN HOLLYWOOD DIDN'T UNDERSTAND WHAT MOTIVATED ME, SO THEY IN TURN TRIED TO GIVE ME HARD TIME. THIS ONLY HAD THE EFFECT OF "WHIPPING" ME TO GREATER HEIGHTS IN MY DETERMINATION TO BE ABLE TO

1

Joy Wilkerson

FULFILL THE WISHES OF MY THOUSANDS OF GI FRIENDS. MEN OF EVERY RANK WANTED ME TO COME TO VIETNAM, BUT THE MEN WHO WERE ABOVE THE RANK OF CAPTAIN WANTED TO BE ANONYNOUS. WHILE ADVISING AND CORRESPONDING WITH ME, THESE SAME HIGHLY RANKED MEN WOULD GO OUT AND BEAT THE BUSHES BEHIND THE SCENES IN ORDER TO LET THE WHOLE WORLD KNOW THAT I WAS VERY MUCH WANTED, AS A FRIEND,

TO BE ALLOWED TO COME TO VIETNAM. IN MOST OF THE LETTERS I RECEIVED FROM THEM, THE MILITARY MEN WOULD ASK WHAT THEY COULD DO TO HELP MAKE MY TRIP TO VISIT THEM A REALITY. LATER, MY FRIENDS FOUND OUT THAT THIS WAS A LARGE AND DIFFICULT TASK, AS I WAS DELIBERATELY BEING HELD BACK BY A FEW, EGO-RIDDEN MEN IN HOLLYWOOD. ONE REPORTER WROTE IN "THE SACRAMENTO BEE" THAT IF JOY WILKERSON WASN'T ALLOWED TO GO TO VIETNAM, THEN ALL OF HOL.LYWOOD WOULD BE DRAGGED ACROSS THE OCEAN.

THE POLITICIANS WOULDN'T ALLOW OUR FIGHTING MEN TO WIN THIS WAR IN VIETNAM AND PEOPLE AT HOME WERE SEEMINGLY PICKETING AGAINST THEM, SO THIS WAS ONE WAR

2

THEY WERE GOING TO WIN! THEY WERE GOING TO BRING THIS 110-POUND BLOND TO VIETNAM. SOME OF THEM TOOK UP A COLLECTION IN DA NANG AND GOT IN TOUCH WITH A TRAVEL

AGENCY: THEY WERE GOING TO SEND FOR ME ON THEIR OWN... AMIDST THIS UPROAR, DALE ROBERTSON, WHEN ASKED BY OUR NEW HOLLYWOOD OVERSEAS PRESIDENT, MR. JIMMY SHELDON, AGREED TO TAKE ME ALONG WITH HIM.

EACH DAY, WHEN MY BAG OF LETTERS ARRIVED AT MY HOUSE, I WOULD SIT DOWN AND READ THROUGH ALL OF THEM, AND THEN I WOULD MARK ON THE ENVELOPE WHETHER IT WAS A FIRST- OR SECOND-TIME-AROUND LETTER. IF IT WAS A SECOND TIME AROUND LETTER I WOULD MAIL MY PEN PAL MY PINK LETTER OF THE WEEK, WHICH I HAD PRINTED AT A STATIONERY STORE. HOWEVER, IF IT WAS A FIRST-TIME LETTER, THEN I WOULD GO TO MY TYPEWRITER AND ANSWER THAT LETTER PERSONALLY. THIS KEPT ME BUSY FROM SUN UP TO WAY PAST SUN DOWN.

THE STORY OF MY USO WORK BEGAN WHILE I WAS SHOOTING A CHRISTMAS TELEVISION SHOW WITH BOB HOPE IN NOVEMBER OF 1965. FIRST, LET ME TELL YOU HOW I GOT TO THE POINT IN MY LIFE WHERE I WAS DOING TELEVISION

SHOWS WITH BOB HOPE AND DANNY THOMAS. IT ALL BEGAN ONE DAY IN 1962, WHEN I SAID TO MYSELF, "JOY, WHY DON'T YOU BECOME A MODEL?" I HAD JUST BEEN LAID OFF FROM MY JOB AT LOCKHEED VAN NUYS, AND PEOPLE WERE FOLLOWING ME AROUND IN SHOPPING MALLS, SAYING, "WOULD YOU LIKE TO BECOME A MODEL?" I WAS THIRTY YEARS OLD AT THE TIME, HAVING HAD THE LAST OF MY THREE CHILDREN BY THE AGE OF 27, AND I THOUGHT "ME?!! I'M THIRTY YEARS OLD!"

WELL, I WENT HOME AND PICKED UP THE PHONE BOOK, AND I DECIDED TO CALL THE POWERS MODELING AGENCY BECAUSE I HAD HEARD OF THAT SCHOOL. IT SOUNDED FAMILIAR.

I CALLED THE SCHOOL AND MADE AN APPOINTMENT FOR THE FOLLOWING SATURDAY. I SHOWED UP FOR MY INTERVIEW DRESSED INCORRECTLY. THE FIRST THING THEY TOOK AWAY FROM ME WAS MY ANKLET, AND I WAS TOLD NEVER TO WEAR WHITE SHOES BECAUSE IF THEY GOT DIRTY YOU WOULDN'T HAVE THE 'BAND BOX' LOOK.

I WENT TO THAT SCHOOL FOR TWO YEARS. BOB GRANT WAS OUR VOICE TEACHER. I NEVER TOOK MUCH NOTICE OF OUR MAKE-UP CLASSES BECAUSE I DIDN'T LIKE TO WEAR

MAKE-UP IN THE FIRST PLACE. I HAD THREE CHILDREN AT HOME AND WAS KEPT VERY BUSY JUST KEEPING UP WITH ALL THE CAR POOLING.

I MUST HAVE BECOME AN AUTHORITY ON HOW TO DRESS BECAUSE MANY PEOPLE WERE ASKING MY ADVICE ABOUT WHAT CLOTHES THEY SHOULD BE WEARING. THAT LED TO MY PUTTING ON FASHION SHOWS AT HIGH QUALITY RESTAURANTS AND THAT, MY FRIENDS, IS HOW I ENDED UP IN SHOW BIZ. I WAS PUTTING ON A DAILY LUNCHEON FASHION SHOW AND I HADN'T PAID ANY ATTENTION TO THE FACT THAT THIS PARTICULAR RESTAURANT, WHICH WAS CALLED "THE CARRIAGE HOUSE", WAS RIGHT ACROSS THE STREET FROM NBC.

FIFTEEN YEARS LATER I MARRIED A MR DWAYNE RATLIFF WHO WAS THE NBC NETWORK CENSOR.

IT WAS DANNY THOMAS WHO PUT ME INTO MY FIRST NETWORK TELEVISION SHOW. MY MOTHER HAD GIVEN ME TRANQUILIZERS BECAUSE I WAS SCARED TO DEATH OF GETTING ON THE STAGE WITH THIS GREAT NETWORK OF SUPER STARS. I KEPT TRIPPING OVER THE CABLES AND CUE CARDS WOULD BE PUT IN FRONT OF MY FACE, WHICH SAID, "JOY, STOP

Joy Wilkerson

LOOKING INTO THE CAMERA"! I WAS IN A SKIT WITH EDDIE ADAMS AND WHAT WITH MY TOTAL LACK OF STAGE TRAINING I CAME OFF AS A COMEDIENNE. WELL, AFTER ALL, I DO SHARE MY BIRTHDAY WITH LUCILLE BALL AND GRACIE ALLEN BIRTHDAY, OR CLOSE TO IT. WE ARE ALL LEOS!

The SEAL Story of: The U.S.O. Show By Chuck Detmer

SEAL Team Two's third platoon was stationed at an old French compound about a mile from Binh Thuy Air Base. For reasons we never knew, our base of less than 100 sailors was to have its own private U.S.O. show.

We didn't expect a Bob Hope extravaganza, but were a little disappointed when, after all the hype, we learned it was a three person show starring Dale Robertson. We didn't have anything against Dale Robertson, we were just wondering what he did besides cowboy. When we found out one of the other two persons was Playboy Bunny Joy Wilkerson, we no longer cared about what Dale was going to do.

The show was to consist of Dale Robertson hosting, a female singer (Joy Llers) doing numbers from a Broadway show that she'd been in, and a Playboy Bunny (Joy Wilkerson), just looking good. Dale was a real down to earth nice guy. He told a couple of jokes, then introduced the singer by saying she was having trouble with her voice. The singer gave it a try but very little came out and she looked as though trying to sing really hurt. Dale stopped her before she lost what little voice she had left. We gave her a hand and thanked her for trying.

Joy Wilkerson

When it looked as though the show was over; Dale said that, with a little encouragement, we might be able to convince Bunny Joy Wilkerson to do a couple of numbers. The singer was a nice looking gal, but we were more interested in eyeballing the Bunny's talents anyway. Joy warned us she wasn't a singer but was willing to try. Boy was she telling the truth! Even with her very obvious assets, when she started to sing all we could do was wince. In order to stop our pain, or maybe to give Joy some relief, Dale cut the song short.

In an effort to give us some kind of a show Dale told us he was going to do a card trick. It sounded to us like the show might hit an even lower low. Dale must have read the disappointment in our faces as he held up his hands to assure us we were going to like the trick. The trick consisted of Dale placing a card on the ground in front of each us and letting Joy, in her low-cut outfit, bend over and pick them up. Since we were all seated on the ground we had a great view. Dale was right, the trick was a huge success.

After the show all three performers hung around and talked. They were all super friendly. It felt good to meet people who cared enough to make the trip and risk the embarrassment of trying to do something just to make a bunch of servicemen happy. The thing we enjoyed the most was that they just hung out with us and talked after the show. We all recognized the fact that these good folks really cared.

8

Dale had a lot of questions about SEALs and what the enemy was like. We told him there was a patrol going out to snatch a prisoner that night and if he had his six-gun that never ran out of bullets, he was welcome to come along. As it turned out Dale was just like the characters he played and jumped at the chance. The base C.O. got word of what was going on and insisted Dale get out of the boat before it could get underway.

The C.O. looked at us in disbelief and asked if we were out of our minds. We told him we weren't stupid, Dale

Robertson was going to stay in the boat.. For some reason our answer didn't convince the C.O. that we weren't stupid.

The snatchers on the op were Larry Bailey, Lenny Waugh, Bill Goines, Ken Estok, Harry Mattingly and a VN Sgt. named Thanh. After hitting three empty hootches they came upon four sleeping V.C. in the same hootch and decided to take all four back. The prisoners were tied, gagged, brought back to the boat, blindfolded and transported back to base.

The prisoners were put into an extra room at the compound before being transported to Sa Dec. We saw Dale the next morning and he asked if he could see what Viet Cong looked like.

While on the way to see the prisoners the girls appeared and asked to come along too. You know we didn't say no to them. We felt bad about dragging the prisoners out all muddy, bound, gagged and blindfolded, so we cleaned them up as best we could We didn't want to shock the girls so we even took the gags and blindfolds off the prisoners before letting the girls see them. When our guests asked if they could take pictures of the prisoners, things really got out of hand. Before it was over it looked more like a family reunion than a combat operation. I still wonder what those V.C. thought after being snatched, bound, gagged and blindfolded only to find themselves being photographed the next morning with two luscious babes. Talk about the fortunes of war; those poor guys had a great war stop which I'm sure, no one ever believed.

More about Joy _

JOY WILKERSON- Actress, Racer, Talk Show Hostess. Joy Wilkerson was named as one of the "Two Thousand Women of Achievement-i 971". She was one of the few women

In 1963, quite by chance, I fell right smack in the middle of a show biz career. I was considering jumping out of this somewhat-less-than-successful profession into a more sane type of life, when I found myself flat on my back in a hospital, having just had a very unglamorous appendectomy. I was hating every moment of it, for confinement and idleness is something I have always tried to avoid, especially if it is enforced.

During moments of depression and feeling sorry for myself because of my predicament, along with the fact that my much-loved father had just passed away, I reluctantly picked up the daily paper to see what was going on in this wide world without me. My eyes fell upon a heart-rending story, splashed all over the front page of the paper, concerning the dilemma the 101st Airborne Division was in at that very moment. Then, on the second page, I read specifically about a Colonel Emerson and his men who had been under fire from the VC on a rather bloody hill, for the past thirty-six hours.

At last my mind stopped dwelling on my "poor self" and it started to contemplate the plight that our fighting American men were having in Vietnam, and all over Vietnam for that matter, not just on one particular hill. Funny how, until this moment in my life, Vietnam had just seemed such a remote place to me, as if it truly hadn't existed at all. I had no inkling that I was to become a "mama-san" in Vietnam. I have always been a softhearted person, but my charitable feelings had only ever extended to children and animals. Within days I had packaged together some of my publicity pictures, would-be "dumb blond" actress that I was (the dumb blond type was the way I appeared in television and films), plus a nice, cheery note written in open letter form to all the members of the 101st Airborne Division, and addressed it to Colonel Emerson, Vietnam.

Sometime during the year of 1965 I picked up an astrology book from a local bookstore, and I read that it was now predicted for my astrological sign

11

to be busy in the field of communication. Quite frankly, I considered this to be a bunch of "poppycock", so I had a good laugh and promptly forgot the whole incident. At that time I wasn't even doing a good job of writing to my mother, who resided in San Diego, California. This was soon to change and I would be recruiting my mother and any other family member I could find to help me in addressing hundred of envelopes daily. I continued going about my business of trying to set the world of Hollywood on fire, for want of any other activity, when one day a letter arrived from a Lieutenant named Jack. He was writing to me on behalf of Colonel Emerson, telling me about all the fun times that the 101st Airborne Division had had upon the arrival of my letter and the girl-next-door pin-up pictures, now that they were off that darn hill. Lieutenant Jack thanked me most graciously and stated just how much everybody in the 101st Airborne Division had appreciated my thoughtfulness. It seems that the men of this division had had a party where they had raffled off my pictures, and a much-deserved fun time was had by one and all.

I immediately answered this most kind letter from Lieutenant Jack and we became pen pals, since he wanted to break into show biz himself. He was killed in action on another hill, six weeks later. I cried for two days over a man I had never met. Unbeknownst to me, my life of communicating with and on behalf of our military had just begun. My 101st Infantry friends had one of my pictures placed in their company newspaper, "The Diplomat and the Warrior", and a member of the 1st Infantry Division, "The Big Red One", managed to get my agency address off one of my photos. He wrote to me, requesting that I please send some photos to "The Big Red One", and of course I complied.

For about four weeks I wrote daily to my ever-growing list of military pen pals. I was sending them records, books and general information about what was going on in the States. Many GIs wanted to hear about the latest men's fashion so that before returning home they could have some clothes made in Hong Kong, while they were on an R and R (Rest and Recreation). One day my mailman, who liked to whistle "There's No Business like Show Business" when he reached my doorstep, rapped at my door and yelled, "Joy, where do you want me to put all of this?". I yelled back, "Put what?" and my mailman said, "These four mailbags filled with letters that are addressed to you from overseas!" Well, ladies and gentlemen, my years of communicating started that day, in all their glory. It seemed that the "Big Red One" had been instrumental in having my picture, which I had autographed to them, placed in a spot of honor in the "The Stars and Stripes", and it was destined to appear in such a spot in different issues over the next six months. As you may or may not know, this popular military newspaper goes to all branches of the military that are stationed on all four "Godforsaken" corners of the earth.

Multiple numbers of mailbags were destined to show up on my doorstep for the next five years and, believe it or not, the year 1971 still found me to be the Dear Abby of the military. The general issue on everyone's minds, on that first day of many thousands of letters, was the question of "what is wrong with the Marines?" "What is wrong with the Air Force?" "What is wrong with the Seabee's, Green Berets, Huey Helicopter Pilots, Signal Corp, 9th Army, 5th Army, Tank Battalion...", and so on and so on and so on. This was my first encounter with the healthy competition that exists between all the many varying and much-needed military branches. From that day forth I spent my life from 6:00 AM to 10:00 PM every day, writing to my newfound friends and telling them just how much I truly appreciated the job they were doing for all of us still here at home. This schedule included all holidays, and I happily gave up all social life and professional pursuits.

It seemed that in just the time it takes to blink your eyes, my picture was appearing in all the military papers, underscored with all my new 113 titles: I was "Miss This" or "Miss That". In that first year alone I received literally thousands of much-cherished titles and plaques. The next question I received from my great mass of pen pals was "why didn't I come to Vietnam to entertain them?" I wrote back that, yes, I had done a few Stateside USO shows at local military hospitals, but I had a "Betty Boop"-type voice and I didn't see that they would find this particularly entertaining.

My overseas friends said they didn't care if I sounded like Mickey Mouse, and would I please come to Vietnam? Just like that, folks! It seemed like a fairly simple request, since I had been reading in the newspapers that entertainers were greatly needed everywhere to work and travel for the US0. Thinking it over for about thirty seconds, I flew to my typewriter and wrote to my friends. I wrote a letter of the week and had it printed. I sent it to my thousands of pen pals, saying that I would dearly love to visit all of them in Vietnam, but that they should expect, as far as my singing ability went, the "Miss Miller" of the war.

I confidently called up the VIPs of the Hollywood Overseas Committee (HOC) and informed them about my desire to volunteer my services for an overseas USO show to Vietnam. Lo and behold, I was promptly but politely turned down with the statement - true though it was - that I simply wasn't a famous enough name or big enough talent for the United State government to send to a war zone. The only way you could be a nobody and go to a war zone was to join the service. It was suggested to me by the HOC that perhaps if I appeared in a Las Vegas show they would consider that to be an audition, on my part, for a Vietnam USO tour. The only problem was that it would cost about fifty thousand dollars or more to put an act together for a show in Las Vegas. Not only was I an unknown, but I was a poor unknown to boot.

As it turned out, with the help of the press all over the world, who had heard of my plight (my stock was picking up), I had that audition for the HOC and I had it right here in Hollywood. It took three tranquilizers for me to get the courage just to show up with my piano player friend, let alone sing. My only other offer was from a nightclub owner, who suggested that I become an "exotic dancer" and dance my way to Asia. The Hollywood Overseas Committee told the members of the press that I would either be "the biggest bomb or the biggest bombshell" to hit Vietnam.

My military friends bequeathed the title of "Miss South Vietnam" (though I don't look very Asian) upon me, and the news media pitched in to help, writing great masses of stories, which appeared world wide, and gathering me a wee bit of world renown. Voila!

Six months later, in April of 1967, still with my seeming lack of fame, I was on my way to Asia with the mighty fine actor who went by the name of Dale Robertson. I bet you've heard of him, right? Since up to this point I had only been a "hothouse" type of female, strictly California style, I truly didn't know what I was in for on this trip. When I landed in the Philippines in my chic, hot pink wool dress with matching shoes and a white leather coat, the first thing the knowledgeable stewardess told me was that once I left the comfort of the airplane, my hairdo would promptly go straight (the bobby pins even rusted my blond hair) and my make-up would run right off my face. This stewardess knew what she was talking about, and so did the military nurses, who were all sensibly dressed. By the time we reached the air terminal, a luxury we wouldn't find later in Vietnam, I felt and looked like an over-the-hill stripper. An hour or so after this non-beautifying experience, I landed in Cahm Rahn Bay, Vietnam. We had to stay clear of Saigon, where "Charlie" was kicking up a fuss. The way I looked when I landed in Vietnam, service men were asking me why I didn't look like my pictures. Ha! The only way I could have done that would have been to go back home. The heat in Cahm Rahm Bay really got to me and I pleaded with the nice officer who met our flight, to please find a place for me where I could change my clothes. Now this officer and I looked like we had just stepped out of the film "Lawrence of Arabia", because he carried me, baggage and all, knee deep through white sand to the closest nurses' quarters, which was minus a powder room. I guess, what with all that sand, there was no need for a powder room. My fashionable patent pumps weren't a good choice for Asia, out in Tooleyville; consequently, at that moment I found myself to be more of a liability than a help to our fighting men.

Boy, was I refreshed once I had slipped into a cool mini-dress and boots (what else?) and replaced my sun-streaked and caked makeup with just a

17

dab of moisture cream. At that very moment I truly appreciated the well-wishing friend who had put some Handi-wipes into my purse. I topped off the transformation in my appearance by pulling back my somewhat lost curls with a ribbon. The only talents you need to be a hit in Vietnam with our boys are to be a good sport, don't complain, and look like a girl.

Dale and I were happily launched on a three-week tour of Vietnam doing two and three shows daily, in the rain for the most part, with a couple of fellows holding a rain poncho over me, while I sang and danced and answered rather personal questions such as was I a 36-23-34? Dale didn't shave or truly clean up until we hit Hawaii on our way home, because he sat up nightly, after I had retired, and laughed and joked and played cards with all of his new-found buddies. The water supply in the military compounds in Vietnam is wisely turned off at 10:00 PM, so Dale had great difficulty connecting with any of it. I myself would be escorted to a male latrine, for they didn't have any use in building female latrines, and a big sign would be placed on the door that a female was washing out a few things, such as herself! In the morning, the only way I could get these busy war-fighting men to remember my toiletry needs was to station myself, negligee, toothbrush, and hair rollers in front of the male latrine and sit prettily until some very astonished male ran across me and rushed around getting all other males to fallout and let me briefly have the run of the place.

18

Sometimes there would be some Vietnamese male servant in the washroom, working as a custodian, who didn't understand why I wanted him removed also. There seemed to be a lot of togetherness in the "Powder Room" habits of the Asian folks, or, I might add, the lack of bathroom habits.

The way the Vietnamese crept around in my room at night unnerved me more than the lizard that was placed in my quarters, whose primary duty was to eat the insects who were trying, in turn, to eat me.

On my day off, because the army figured a girl needed to wash her hair, I was flown to the boondocks (due to movie insurance reasons Dale had to stay in a safe area, however), meaning the bush country - and when I landed in Vietnam I thought I already was in the boondocks! Here our men slept in small, wet tents, and I was marched out amongst the rubber trees and a rain poncho was held in place while I treated this rubber tree as though it were my indoor plumbing. When the GIs came across me in my hair rollers I would apologize, but they in turn said that it was just OK by them, for it reminded them of their own round-eyed girls back home.

One Captain, a Huey helicopter pilot, had asked me out to dine with him, but our tour didn't go to his particular area in Vietnam. There was also the fact that there was a 10:00 PM curfew and the war department wouldn't let me out of its sight. He sent me all the fixings for our supposed dinner get-together: taped music, candles and C-rations. On the tape were four Huey pilots singing an original song, just for me. I still have that tape.

Dale and I had the exciting opportunity to fly to some American aircraft carriers. You have not lived until you have had the chance to make a landing aboard one of these ships, sitting backwards - how else in the very small aircraft? - when a giant hook seems to reach out and grab the plane. I hate to think about when these hooks miss. I was told that this happened on rare occasions. Dale and I visited the USS Ticonderoga and the USS Bonnie Dick, and we could also see the USS Kitty Hawk close by, floating majestically on the Asian waters. The men aboard these aircraft carriers treated us with the usual military graciousness, and we were fed magnificently, as always. The cook aboard the USS Ticonderoga even made a foot-high cake for us.

I will tell you that during one USO show my guitarist and I became separated and he was playing one song and I was singing another, and the sailors didn't even notice. I consider that to be an example of how much the men overseas appreciate their USO shows.

For want of something to do the GIs love to take your picture and they don't care if it is just from the neck down. In good-natured retaliation, Dale bought himself a camera at one of the PXs and when the GIs took his picture, he would slip out his camera and take theirs.

20

On the subject of pictures, if a girl goes to Vietnam just to look for a husband then she might as well forget it, for ninety percent of the men in the Armed Forces that I met were happily married and, without asking them to, they would whip out pictures of their loved ones back home. The only event that takes preference over a USO show is mail call!

I would like to state that while in Vietnam you acquire the habit of waving and saying hi to every American you see, because all Americans overseas are so happy just to see one another, and that is all it takes to be one big, happy family. Upon my return home, for many months to come, I found myself waving to everyone while driving on the freeway, even just traveling up and down city elevators.

I took three pairs of pantyhose with me, but luck was with me: my original pair held up and I was still wearing them, a bit baggier at the knee, when I arrived back at Travis Air Base, San Francisco, three weeks later.

There was no time for me to be color-coordinated during my USO tour, so I decided that if I had to plan a future trip I would just take a suitcase of clothes all in one color. This would save save me time and I would not be forever searching for the right-colored pixie band to go with this or that outfit.

Before I left on my USO tour, it was suggested to me by the HOC (Hollywood Overseas Committee) that I take along some false hair, for emergencies. If I had taken the time to worry about anything false I would have missed my transportation and been left in the middle of some swamp somewhere. My hair began to look so false all by itself – bleached blondes don't wear well in the Asian heat – that one GI in the mess hall came up and playfully pulled the back of my hair to see if it would come off.

I stayed healthy through all the rigors of the trip, since just before leaving the States I had received a lifetime of immunization shots in just one week. I also attribute it to the canned milk that I carried in my suitcase. Dale missed not having milk so much that he threatened to buy a cow. I would gladly have shared my milk with Dale, but we were rushed around so much from show to show and spot to spot that I couldn't get my suitcases closed before I was being lifted on to another chopper and whisked off to a new base, where the men were all so eager to say hi to this rain-soaked girl who stood before them.

The night of the show for the "Big Red One" and the 101st Airborne Division was an especially emotional one for me, for those were the men who had started the whole chain of events. It seemed that I cried with sentiment through the whole show. Afterwards, all the men who could fit on the stage climbed up there with me and gave me their official black scarves as my very own, and we all sat down onstage for a good cry and gossip session.

When you land in Vietnam you are assigned a military escort who stays with you and has command over you through thick and thin. Our personal escort turned out to be a very efficient member of the Special Forces named Jim, and when he said "jump" we just asked how high! We trusted his judgment completely. We were to listen to this outstanding member of the Green Berets at all times, and he certainly made Dale and I feel that he was our "security blanket". This Special Forces man of ours had just about two words for all occasions: "Affirmative" and "Negative".

The military was most gracious in asking me if I needed anything washed, and I replied, "Oh, how I wish I had something that you could wash!", for dummy me had shown up in a war zone with a wardrobe full of non-washable clothes that could only be dry-cleaned. If my Green Beret hadn't sought out what seemed to be the only dry-cleaners – and you could use the term loosely – in Vietnam, I would have been a sorry sight for most of my trip. Also Jim needed to remind Dale and I to take our weekly quinine pills. In addition, if you managed to get the "tourista" – and everybody managed this – then our problem-solving Green Beret came up with some pills to cure the "trots".

For security reasons, most people have never heard of our highly trained and little-talked-about Navy Seals. I was fortunate to spend some time with them, and it was a most delightful and surprising evening. With Dale's permission, and unbeknown to me, at the end of the show on this one particular evening, a group of Navy Seals in full war paint captured me in fun, trying to scare me, and they ran with me in their arms, rifles on their backs, down to the Mekong Delta River boats. Nobody had informed my Special Forces man of the hoax, so he came charging after us, knowing he had complete and full responsibility from General Westmorland to make certain that Dale and I were under his wing, so to speak, and protected at all times.

The next morning at breakfast I met these same Navy Seals, back in full dress uniform. For security reasons I won't go into their activities the night before, once I had retired, but I will tell you that these men make America stand tall. I later heard that, upon my leaving this Navy base, the men cut up my bed sheets and raffled off the strips of sheeting for beer money.

Because I was traveling with a personality as well-known as Dale Robertson, I was always being ushered into the VIP room at the various airports. While in Guam, seeking some American type of refreshment, such as a malt or hamburger, I slipped out from this particular room. Just for the fun of it I got into a long line of humanity, not knowing what I would find at the other end, hoping it was an ice cream parlor, but, non-drinker though I was, I ended up buying eight bottles of scotch. In Guam alcohol was tax-free so everybody bought it. When I got home I threw the eight bottles of scotch under my bed to use later as Christmas presents.

I had such difficulty in trying to eat while in Vietnam because of the intense heat that my Special Forces escort started to worry about me and he would nag me to eat something. However, by the time I landed back in San Francisco, I was a very hungry female. Dale was a doll for he spent his last fifty cents in cash buying a tomato juice for me. Our airplane didn't serve malts!

The HOC cautioned entertainers not to take much money with them on a USO tour and what money Dale and I had with us we spent during our last evening in Saigon, shopping for souvenirs for our families back home. Shopping in Vietnam is like shopping in Mexico – you bargain a lot. Dale and I, being unfamiliar with the Vietnamese currency, were never certain just how much an object was costing us, and we still don't know.

The only trouble I caused my entertainer friend Dale Robertson was when we landed in Hawaii, on our way home. I discovered I had misplaced my precious passport, having unwisely used it as a bookmarker during the trip. Dale thought he would have to leave me locked up in the official office of the air terminal in Hawaii until Washington D.C. cleared me, giving permission for me to return home. Luckily, in the nick of time, having put the airport in an uproar, the book housing my most precious document was found under the seat where I sat, and now we were on the final lap of our trip home. I must see Hawaii someday, as it looked beautiful from the air.

Upon arriving home I had the usual American craving and I considered it a bit of luck to find an all-night restaurant while driving home from the Los Angeles International airport with my mother in tow, in the wee hours of the morning. My mother had cried when I left for Vietnam, and now here she was, picking up her tanned, healthy and hungry daughter.

During my first week home I was still oriented to Saigon time, so I slept days and paced the house at night. In the second week home the pacing stopped, for I had seemingly come down with every available virus that Vietnam had to offer a foreigner. The third week home I was thoroughly bored with life in California and missed the fact that I no longer had to tuck in my mosquito netting tightly around my bed at night. I wanted to return to Vietnam pronto! It just seemed that I was so very needed there.

Since my trip to Vietnam I have been lecturing to many clubs around the USA about my experiences in the country, and I like to speak with levity. I don't profess to know or understand whether we should have troops in Vietnam or not, but I do know that as long as Americans are there, then that is where I want to be too!!

Right now I'm busily trying to help the POW organization and, believe me, they can use all the help they can get. I have accepted the fact that I just don't have the time or the inclination to continue to pursue a full time show biz career, and I am not interested in fame or fortune; consequently I shall never, I know, go to a war zone out of anything but love for my country.

True story by Joy Wilkerson in 1971 about her trip to Vietnam, April 1967

Joy calls her story "Look, Ma, I'm Communicating".

Joy Wilkerson

NOTES TAKEN DURING TRIP TO VIETNAM, APRIL OF 1967

In April of 1967 at LAX airport I was handed a steno pad from a friend, so here goes! While on my USO trip I'm going to take notes about this adventure.

April 12 Went to LAX airport with my daughter Candy and my mother at 3:30 P.M. Dale Robertson and ten people from the paper "The Entertainer" came at 4:00 PM. We took pictures constantly until 5:15 PM, when I was the last person rushed onto the plane. We took off for Frisco at 5:30. Gypsy Boots gave me candy and fruit bars to take with me to Vietnam and Jim Depue did a radio interview with me.

We landed at San Francisco Airport and were met and interviewed by NBC Television news. We also televised meeting a long line of military men, one by one. After signing dozens of autographs Dale and I went to dinner, paid for by the USO. San Francisco was so cold! We then took a two-hour drive to Travis Airport Base where we sat and watched television for two hours, after which we boarded our plane.

First stop Hawaii, where we landed at 4:55 AM Stateside time. In Hawaii it was 2:55 AM. It was warm in Hawaii and beautiful. The stores in the airport were open all night. We only stayed for twenty minutes and since I had just gotten my period, I spent the time washing out my underpants in

28

the bathroom. Next stop was the Philippines, after a ten-hour flight. Besides Dale and I and our 2 musicians, the plane was filled with GIs and two nurses. The nurses ate every meal offered them, which I skipped, as they said when they were flying home they never had time to eat, because they were taking care of those who had been wounded in Vietnam. The nurses make this flight to the Philippines three times a month. Sometime this plane is so cold that I'm very grateful I'm wearing a wool dress.

We just left Hawaii, where it was early Thursday morning, and in two hours we passed the dateline and then it became Friday AM.

After a ten-hour flight to the Philippines we took a five-hour flight to Cahm Rahn Bay, Vietnam, where we are landing instead of Saigon, for safety precautions. From Cahn Rahn Bay it's a thirty mile drive to Saigon. Gee, I hope I find a bed and bath there!!

I slept on the plane for five hours, then rehearsed. Plus I was invited to sit in the cockpit with the three pilots while we landed in the Philippines and boy, was it hot! Departing the plane I look wilted and droopy!! At the Manila Air Base I sent a postcard to my mom while my hair went limp. Might as well give it up with my hair, and I took out pixie bands to at least keep my hair out of my eyes. Now it was 5 PM in Los Angeles, but in the Philippines it was 8:30 AM. Thursday, the next day, we landed in Cahm Rahn Bay, where I changed into a cooler dress and I danced and visited with all the military men. A Lt. Biggs looked out for me, after which we had an hour and a half flight to Saigon in an non-pressurized plane.

I tried to call a Major Jarvis, one of my pen pals, but he was gone for the day, flying a Huey Helicopter.

It is hot in Vietnam. We met our protocol Captain at the Officer's Club, and finally went to bed.

The cast from Peyton Place had been trying to return to the States for three days and shared our hotel for a day. Our lodging was a big suite which consisted of three bedrooms and bathrooms. In front of the hotel were sand bags and military police on alert behind them.

Everybody wears pajamas, and the girls wear long, violet dresses over their pajamas. Traffic consists of bicycles and motorcycles and the traffic rule is that the biggest vehicle wins the right of way. This country is beautiful and so are the women.

On Saturday we entertained the troops at 2 PM in Nha Bay. The troops laughed and enjoyed our show. Later that same day we had dinner and entertained the 199th M.P. Battalion, and it rained. It rained every day at around 2 and 7 PM A Mr. Coroy of the USO was there, as well as a Col. Frank Hill.

Sunday we flew by plane to Saigon and then onto Binh Thuy to visit the US Special Forces USFF, and from there we were on our way to Cantho for a l:30 show. We met a Lt. Commander Bob Cosgrove and then we were on our way again to Binh Thuy at the Mekong Delta. It is becoming almost impossible for me to keep up with my note-writing because it seems that I'm constantly being lifted off and onto a Huey Helicopter or a C-130 plane. Dale wanted to know why we were always crisscrossing Vietnam by plane or helicopter, and why didn't we just go in one straight line. We were told that we had to be sent wherever "Charley" wasn't too active at that time.

We were now with the Navy Seals. A Lt. Commander Charles Billings sang with us on stage. I had a snack at the officer's club with some of the Navy Seals, and I remember one in particular by the name of Lt. Larry Bailey from Texas. I truly cared for Lt. Bailey, as I did for all of my pen pals. Later I learned that Lt. Bailey had been killed.

The Navy Seals were going out on a night patrol and they were made up in what appeared to me to be Halloween makeup. Well, these Navy Seals kidnapped me right off the stage towards the end of the show as a joke, agreed upon by Dale Robertson earlier, and did it come as one big surprise, but fun!! I wasn't at all frightened, as who could be frightened while in the arms of those most capable men?

The next morning a Major came and got me from my room in order to take me to see the four captured VC (Viet Cong) that they had caught in a house the night before. The boys who had playfully kidnapped me during

31

our USO show the night before had captured these four VC after I had gone to bed. I was told that the youngest VC cried all night. But I might add that the VC hate to be captured by the Vietnamese soldiers, who rough them up, and especially since the VC had hung a Vietnamese Major a few nights before. My military friends confided in me that usually the Vietnamese soldiers would just run away and leave the fighting for our military men from the USA. I was told later via mail from a Navy man whose room I used while in the Mekong Delta, that he cut up my bed sheets in six-inch squares and sold them for one dollar each, which he used for beer money.

Next Dale and I did shows for the 22nd TASS in the afternoon and met a Colonel Bob and a Colonel Darran. Later we went to see the Army in Delta at Cantho and did an evening USO show. General Bill Desobry escorted me to the stage and then Dale, the General and I had drinks and visited till 1 AM. Since the water was turned off at 10 PM, I excused myself for a little while in order to wash out my pantyhose. I don't know what I drank as I didn't drink alcohol! After I had gone to bed I could see this General Bill Desobry dancing by himself, so I went over to where he was and spoke to him, and he told me that you didn't know just who "Charlie" was, be it the daytime Vietnamese who worked in the kitchen, or the one who shaved you, because at night the war would start again and some Vietnamese would change into their black pajamas and would then be recognizable as VC. This General said he didn't feel that he had slept very well for eight months, and so he danced and looked at pictures of his wife. He was looking forward to seeing her on his R and R in Japan when his year of duty was up.

The next day was Tuesday and we flew from Contho to Saigon by plane, and then took a helicopter to Long Binh to do a 2:30 show for the Second Field Force in Vietnam. During our flight to Long Binh we flew over an area while bombs were being dropped. It was so sad to think that our American boys were being killed.

Still on Tuesday, at 4 PM, we found ourselves flying to the First Division. We could see a VC prison below us. Boy, did the First Division make me happy by making arrangements for a female room and bath, all for me, though there always seemed to be some Vietnamese person creeping around in my quarters while I was trying to sleep after tucking in the mosquito netting.

At Phuc Vihn we had dinner with First Inf. Colonels Bill and Ron. After dinner we did a show while hearing the sound of big gunfire, which sounded to me like thunder. Dale must have been concerned, as he forgot some of the words to his song. We were told as long as you hear the gunfire you're OK, because when the fire is incoming you don't hear it at all till it arrives.

At the end of the show I cried like a baby out of sentiment over my First Division men, who were absolutely so sweet. Chaplain Assistant David Pearson came up to me and told me that my pen pal Bill Golden had just phoned, so I just kept on crying because of the love and respect that was always there between my military pen pals and myself.

The next day I washed my hair with water from the slow, leaky faucet, and I doubt that I slept at all the way those big guns were going off constantly. I wondered when our military men slept!

On Wed. AM I took a chopper out to the bush country to see the men of the First Inf. Division, who were living in small, wet tents. The first stop was to visit the 28th Inf., which was part of the First Inf. My Green Beret and I took a jeep to visit Med Calf, where the doctors and men go to visit and treat the Vietnamese and pass out goodies. The Vietnamese women just stared at my blond hair, and all of them seemed friendly. They smiled at me, with their mouths red from chewing the drug made from betel nuts. I noticed that many of the Vietnamese people were missing their teeth.

I had lunch with our military men, then I pulled one of their sleeves and said, "Where is the Powder Room?" This man then said, "Captain," and went for help as to what to do with me. The problem was solved when I was marched out amongst the rubber trees and a rain poncho was held in front of me.

My American men friends said that after you have been in Vietnam about three months, you learn to do what the Vietnamese do, and that is just go to the bathroom anywhere and in front of anyone. The children didn't wear diapers: they just ran around with their bare bottoms exposed, saving the use of diapers. Mama-san would wash dishes in the same river people used as a toilet. That is why we Americans had to take medicine so as not to catch anything that we hadn't built up a resistance to. We were cautioned not to eat any fruit or vegetables that the Vietnamese put out to sell. I must say, before five AM if I were near Saigon, I could hear the people chattering. Also, if there was a car in town the Vietnamese men were all over it in wonderment.

Well, I digress. After my lunch with the First Inf. in the bush country, my Green Beret noticed some activity that he felt was suspicious and dangerous, so he rushed me to the jeep and then to a helicopter. Later he told me that he felt the VC were out to kidnap me. The very sad part of this story was that two of my friends that I had left behind were killed, one of them beheaded. I was also told that when the young man was sent home, his head had been put back on his body with wax, and the family was not told about the beheading.

Then we were sent to see Charley and Bravo Company, and I spoke to Alpha Company on the phone from Bravo Company. After that we took a chopper back to Phuc Vihn, and a young military man gave me his black scarf and ring.

A General Hollingsworth asked me to stay in Vietnam with the troops after the rest of the troops from our show had gone home. My answer was I didn't think the War Department would allow me to stay. I didn't even bother to ask Dale about it, because I knew the answer would be no!!

That evening I ate in the enlisted men's mess hall and I visited all the clubs of the First Inf.. All the clubs were decorated in red leather. I was interviewed on tape by the press, and pictures were taken of me in my bathing suit.

On Thursday we took a chopper to Cu Chi to do a show for the 25th Inf. Div. Dale told me I should stay back stage and not go out front before the show started, so what I was wearing should be a surprise, but I just couldn't resist talking to the men who had come to see all of us straight away. I was a dancer, not a singer, but still my fan pen pals came to visit with Dale and I. We weren't in Las Vegas; we were with Americans in a foreign country. The 25th Inf. had their own great band and joined our show.

We then visited a hospital and saw a Colonel Otis. Afterwards, we saw an oil refinery being bombed while we were being transported by chopper to visit the 199th Inf., which seems to be with the 5th Inf. Then we flew to

Lam Son to do a show for the Advisory Group #7 and we were met by a Colonel Jack Walker.

On Friday we took a chopper to visit the 9th Inf. Division Bearcat and I had a press interview. Pictures were taken once again with me in my bathing suit. Dale saw the report on that show and kidded me about it, calling it an obscenity. Later we took a chopper for an evening show to entertain the 199th Light Inf. at Long Binh. I was given a beautiful plaque, but at bedtime I was anxious to leave as we were all bedded down in a trailer, and I was watching the Vietnamese Peeping Toms peep at us!!

The next day we took a plane to the aircraft carrier USS Bon Homme Richard (CVA-31). We were met by Captain Charles Kenneth Ruiz and Admiral Vince DuPuoix. We performed two short shows, which were late, and this was bad news because there the pilots were flying on two different shifts and we had to shorten our shows so that we could entertain all aboard this ship. What happened was that our guitarist, I suppose, didn't understand what songs I had told him I would do, because there wasn't time for me to do all of them. Well, folks, Freddy, our guitarist, was playing one song, and I was singing the other. The incredible thing about this whole mix-up was that the Navy men didn't even seem to notice: they just wanted to know what I was wearing under my mini dress!

Joy Wilkerson

The next morning we flew to the USS Ticonderoga and once again I was photographed in my bathing suit, which was actually the first bathing suit picture that I had already sent to Vietnam and which was put into "The Stars and Stripes". Many bathing suit pictures of me were later put into all of the various military periodicals. A Lt. Sharp of the Air Force (I don't understand why the Air Force was on that ship, but maybe they also flew the fighter planes, along with the Navy pilots) proposed marriage to me, and I found out that he is a Libran. Lt. Sharp went in search of a Chaplain. I also met a Commander Billy Phillips and Dale recommended that when I get back home I date this Commander Billy Phillips. Later, when we were flying home to the USA, I said to Dale, "Thanks a lot, Dale – Commander Billy Phillips has a wife and five children in Memphis, Tennessee!"

Our next stop was Phu Cat, and we were flown there by Navy plane. Here we did an afternoon show for the 37th Tac Fighter Wing and the Red Horse. We did this particular show in the rain and, needless to say, my hair and dress got soaked, even though a raincoat was held over my head by two men.

Next we were flown to Nha Trang for an evening show. I ran into one of my pen pals, who got into trouble for coming to see the show without getting permission from his NCO. I then washed my hair again and had a drink with four Colonels. My drink was usually Coca Cola, because that was

38

what the Vietnamese people were selling all over the place. You could get off a chopper and there would be some Vietnamese vendor, out in Tooleyville, who would want to sell you a Coke.

Now it's Tuesday and it is my one and only day off from doing shows. I skipped breakfast and rested by not getting out of bed till 11 AM. My arms were peeling from the sun. I kept Noxzema on my face, and that was the only thing I put on it, besides two false eyelashes. I had to hold them on for a few minutes to dry because it was so difficult to get them to stick.

On my day off I accepted an offer to take an excursion with a Colonel Curto, after Dale and I had had a long, leisurely lunch. We flew over Big Buda, Cahm Rahn Bay and then to a nearby island to visit Air Force and Army military men. While I was signing autographs and Dale was shooting dice with the troops for drinks, I met a single 38-year-old career pilot named John, born on July 13. Dale then invited John to join us at the Special Forces Officer's Club. I spent my time dancing with everybody.

Our next stop was Ban Me Thuot. We stayed the afternoon and did a show at the Imperial Huntington Lodge. We now flew to Hou Bon for an evening show and we did a show for a very small audience, so Dale closed the show earlier than usual. Afterwards I met one of my pen pals, Bill Golden's cousin.

39

Joy Wilkerson

We stayed the night in the USAID quarters and in the AM we were taken to visit the Montaguard people, who live in trees high above the ground. I don't know who they were; all I was told is they are the mountain people.

After this we flew to see the 4th Inf. at Pleiku and did an evening show at MAVE, which is still in Pleiku. We had a great show at Pleiku for the 4th Inf. Division. Dale and I were each given a crossbow, which brought us a lot of attention later as we strolled though the San Francisco Airport.

On Friday we took a C-130 back to Saigon and we had our departure interview with General McGovern at 4:00 PM. We were presented with certificates of thanks, and also had our pictures taken. Dale and I spent our last night in Saigon shopping for our relatives at home. Captain Ted Lewis paid for the new violet parasol that I loved, as a going away present. It seems like everything in Vietnam was either black or violet. We ran into Ephem Zimbalist Jr. and chatted briefly.

It took us 27 hours to get back to the USA. We left Saigon on April 29, 1967 at 3:00 PM and arrived in Los Angeles at 11:50 PM, and it was still April 29, 1967. We made stops in Guam, Hawaii and Travis Air Force base. The first thing I had in Los Angeles was a malt and hamburger! During our plane trip home, Dale told me that he had written 13 letters to his wife in

40

Los Angeles, and he had simply addressed them to Dale Robertson, Hollywood, California, USA.

It saddened me that our trip and wonderful time with our military friends was over.

Notes were taken by Joy Wilkerson during her trip to Vietnam with Dale Robertson in April 1967.

PARADE ON SECOND STREET, LONG BEACH

BY JOY WILKERSON

June 26, 1966 - My daughter Kim's 8th birthday

I was sitting in Mr. Sam Bern's U.S.O. office when he noticed on his desk a letter he had received from a Mr. Dennis Leslie of Long Beach, requesting some girls who worked for the U.S.O., entertaining service men, to be in a parade. The parade was to be given near Belmont Shores, Long Beach to honor a contractor who had managed to enlarge Second Street in ten weeks instead of six months. Mr. Berns suggested to Mr. Leslie that I be the one to represent the U.S.O. in the parade, and Mr. Leslie never stopped being thrilled by the idea. Somehow the people of Long Beach had got the idea that I had gone to Vietnam with Bob Hope the previous Christmas.

The first thing Mr. Leslie wanted me to do, after he talked to me for three hours on the phone, was have me mail some of my pictures for the Long Beach papers, two of which were the "Dispatch" and the "Long Beach Independent Press and Telegram", to his office at Sixth and Pine Street, Long Beach, California. A few days later pictures of me in a bikini turned up on the front pages of these papers.

The next thing on my agenda was what should I wear in this parade, so I called my agent, Mr. Louis Shurr, but I ended up with making the decision myself. I had a mini length white lace, semi-fitted shift with long sleeves, and a square-cut empire neckline, with a blue velvet ribbon under the bust line, which I had designed, and which my very talented girlfriend Margie made for me.

I was extremely happy with how well that dress held up during the parade. It was just what the doctor ordered. Come to think of it, my agent was known as Doc. Shurr in Hollywood, because there had been a time when he was the only agent in New York, so he was referred to as Louis Shurr, the Doctor of Show Biz. A while later he came to Hollywood with his client, Bob Hope. Doc Shurr was a very kind and caring agent to me. My business manager, Mark Anthony, was assigned by Doc Shurr to advise me. Remember I was a single, out-of-work mother, and getting a $125 dress was a bit out of my budget. Mark Anthony waited for four hours with me for that piece of blue velvet ribbon to arrive. It always appeared to be a big issue between Mark Anthony and Doc Shurr about what was I going to wear, and what age I was supposed to be. I would receive several phone calls a day to discuss these issues. I grew to accept it as a part of Hollywood. Remember up until then I had been a mother in the valley, doing dishes and washing floors!

Mark Anthony wanted me to come to his office and work on some prepared jokes with him for the parade. I didn't make it, so he helped me over the phone later that night, for an hour. By the way, I was never asked to speak. From observing Bob Hope while working with him at NBC, I had learned just how he came to be so popular. As you know, his jokes were always so appropriate for the area he was visiting.

After fighting with my local hairdresser over how he should do my hair, I came home and did it myself. I went to a dinner given by the Immaculate College to honor Bob Hope. Mr. Shurr usually invited me to go to events with he and Bob Hope. I would always chauffeur Doc Shurr because his chauffeur refused to work past 10 PM, and that is the truth! So I would chauffeur Doc Shurr in my white Buick Skylark, and when we would pull up in front of our destination, we would be ignored. This incensed Louis Shurr, but I would say, "Louis, we are not in your limousine!" You see, it was almost impossible to get Louis's limo out of his garage, and he didn't drive. He would walk a couple of blocks to work in Beverly Hills because, get this, his chauffeur wouldn't show up to drive Louis until after 11 AM. As a child, Mr. Shurr had fallen off a swing, and ever since then he had had a thing against anything that moved. Louis told me that one day, when he was at NBC in Burbank, California, Louis didn't have any way to get home (because, of course, his chauffeur wouldn't work past 10 PM). Some kindly

44

person said, "Doc, I'll drive you home – where do you live?" Doc said, "I don't know, but it is close to my office, so just drop me off there."

I was hoping at the Immaculate Heart event that I could pick up some pointers from Bob Hope's speech, but most of the speeches were given by the nuns, and the acoustics were bad. I always carried a few dimes in my cocktail purse, and from time to time Bob Hope would need to borrow some for phone calls at a payphone, which he much preferred to using somebody's office. I suppose it was just more convenient for Bob to hop into a payphone booth.

My business manager, Mark Anthony, and Doc Shurr called me daily to see how things were progressing with my appearance in the parade for the opening of Second Street. Mr. Leslie would call from Long Beach to talk for hours, and tell me how very honored he was to have me in his parade. He would suggest that maybe I could arrange for some publicity photos, on my end, at the time that the helicopter picked me up. I then got on the phone and called up the newspapers. The first paper I called was "The Green Sheet", and they were sure that they had heard of me, and then I called "The Herald Examiner", and they said that they might come. I then called up Harrison Carroll, who turned out to be a good and true friend to me, and he said he couldn't print anything because it was supposed to be televised. The television cameras never came because Belmont Shores couldn't come up

45

with a sponsor. The parade was covered by KMPC radio and the newspapers.

Well, at last the happy day arrived, and I got up at 6:30 AM to do my motherly duties. My mother was going to come by and watch my children. I was to be picked up at 8 AM, and Mr. Leslie called to make certain that I was going to come!! I'm a person of high integrity and I can always be counted on to say what I do and do what I say. I was ready two hours early, which has always been my style. I played cards with the children until it was time to go. My mother drove me to the designated spot and we waited for a half hour, after which I had my mother drive me to a payphone. I called the number I had for Long Beach and was unable to reach anybody, so then I called Information and asked for the phone numbers of all the airports in Van Nuys. I tried to reach the helicopter Sales Manager of Hughes Helicopter Company. Later I called Information again, but I could never find the phone number for the Hughes Helicopter Company. There seemed to have been a mix-up. I was trying to reach a Mr Hoeffer to tell him that I hadn't connected with the men of the press, and we appeared to have lost each other, but then my pilot arrived and, after warming up the helicopter for ten minutes, we took off for Long Beach. We were 45 minutes behind our scheduled arrival.

I found out one thing, and that is that it's impossible to communicate, by voice, in a helicopter. In addition this helicopter only went 85 miles per hour and my make-up was now melting from the heat. I kept asking, "Are we almost there?" but it seemed that we were just passing over Santa Monica. To appease me, I suppose, the pilot handed me a tie clasp in the shape of a helicopter as a souvenir. Finally it looked like we were going to arrive at our destination, which was the Edgewater Inn in Belmont Shores. Much to my surprise, I had a reception committee of cars, photographers, officials, singers, dancers, and buses full of people. I must say there was a big crowd. We landed in a vacant lot next to the hotel and we covered everybody who was waiting for our arrival with a big cloud of dust. The part of this lot that wasn't dusty was muddy, but we muddled through it all in order to take both still and motion pictures.

The pilot was invited to join us for lunch, but said he had other commitments. Remember it took him ten minutes to warm up his helicopter. Before the pilot took off the rest of us rushed out of the area in order to avoid another dust bath.

I jumped into my decorated Cadillac convertible, complete with a very honored chauffeur, who said he had seen me getting on a plane with Bob Hope.

My windblown self was then driven to the front of the hotel, where I was to have luncheon before the parade, with the judges, officials and their wives. This was a very quick lunch as we were now running an hour behind time. My honored chauffeur was waiting in the convertible, ready to whisk me off to the parade site.

However, before I left the hotel I made a quick trip to the powder room to try and repair my hair as best I could. Finally my chauffeur and I were off to the parade site, where I learned that a hundred Marines had been bused in from El Toro and Camp Pendleton to escort me. These Marines had been waiting who knows how long, but I was so thrilled to meet them. At my request, their Captain selected one of the Marines to ride in the convertible with me. This young Marine was a Corporal named Chester, and he told me just how proud he was of his buddies and how he had taught them all they knew.

By the way, there were signs on both sides of my convertible, printed in red and black, which said things like, "Joy Wilkerson, Miss Hollywood Herself, star of the U.S.O., Bob Hope and Red Skelton." It was probably news to Bob Hope and Red Skelton that I was a star in their shows. Yes, I had made appearances in those television shows, but I hadn't thought of myself as a star. Maybe in some eyes just being on television turns you into a star!

My one hundred Marine escorts marched in front of my slowly driven convertible, and I waved to one and all. My blushing young Marine friend, sitting next to me, saluted everyone, but took offense if somebody called out to him as him being a soldier.

I must say it was extremely thrilling to be referred to as a star, photographed, waved to and hollered at in a very friendly way by everybody at the parade site.

At the end of the parade I kissed my young Marine who had traveled with me in the convertible good bye, and I tried to fix him up with the young lady who was the local queen of the parade. The officials of the parade tried to fix Corporal Chester up with me for a photographed date that night, and he was most anxious to comply, but the Captain of the group of marching Marines nixed it by saying that Corporal Chester didn't have the right pants to wear with him; he only had his marching pants. I suppose the Captain wanted his Corporal to wear his dress blues if he was to be photographed on a date with me, the Starlet!

By this time my chauffeur was terribly hot but still very honored!! He hadn't been able to figure out how to turn off the heater in the car. The only physical effect driving in this convertible had had on me was that both of my legs had fallen asleep.

The reason all these Marines had been brought to be in the parade was that I had told Mr. Dennis Leslie about all my pen pal fan mail, and he thought it would be nice to have one of my pen pals from Vietnam escort me in the parade. Since there hadn't been time for him to get an escort from the Vietnam war zone, Mr. Leslie decided to try to get a Lt. Henry Harvey who had recently written to me, and who had given his address as Camp Pendleton. Lt. Henry Harvey could not be found at Camp Pendleton, because it turned out that he was now in Vietnam. Consequently one hundred Marines were sent in his place to be in the Long Beach Parade for the opening of Second Street.

I must say I was overwhelmed and greatly surprised to have one hundred Marines come and join me in Long Beach.

Now since there weren't any Marines at the parade who were wearing the correct pants for a photographed date, and a helicopter pilot and photographer had been flying overhead, shooting pictures (I don't know whether they were still shots or motion pictures), I decided to let my still most-honored chauffeur drive me home in my still-decorated Cadillac. I did show him how to turn off the heater in our loaned Cadillac, however.

Before we left for my home, I stopped by the Edgewater Inn to say goodbye to the officials and their wives and tell them that I was now on my way home. I asked Mr. Clint Repp, before we entered the freeway, to please put the top up on the convertible. My chauffeur offered to drive me anywhere I wanted to go that day and evening, saying he wasn't in any hurry. Nobody knew that I had children, and I was now anxious to get home and relieve my mother of her baby sitting. The trip home took about the same length of time as the helicopter earlier that day.

On my arrival home Mr. Clint Repp, upon my request, said that he would be happy to send me a dozen or so copies of all the newspapers that carried stories about the Long Beach Parade.

I retrieved all the decorations from the convertible to save for posterity, so that I could remember the day I was a star.

When I walked into my house, I found all of my three children crying and saying, "Grandmother drowned the babies in our swimming pool!" It seems that the hamster, which my daughter Kimberly had been given on a television show and which she had named Chippy, not knowing if she had a male or female, had given birth that day. My mother, feeling that I had enough babies to care for, had drowned the newborn babies.

This is how my most unforgettable day ended.

This is a true story written by Joy Wilkerson

Joy Wilkerson

FAST FORWARD FROM APRIL 1967 TO APRIL 1975: JOY VISITS JAPAN

A TRUE STORY BY JOY WILKERSON

I spent those years still devoted to my work with the USO and tried, once again, to be allowed to go to Vietnam.

All of my efforts were for nought, but I did continue working on behalf of the USO and I continued to write to my military pen pals. One in particular, a Sgt. Cummings, kept sending gifts to me for my birthday, Christmas and even on Mothers Day. I'm still using the toaster he sent me..

During those eight years I continued making films, doing television shows and speaking around the USA about what was going on in Vietnam.

In l970 I embarked on a career as a professional race car driver. I attended three racing schools and acquired my licenses to drive in Nascar, Scca and Usac races, and the auto racing insurance company approved my entering into the world of racing with full credentials.

In the spring of 1975, I was dining with my best friend in this world, Doctor Robert Watanabe, and a host of his friends, at a Japanese restaurant, of course, sitting on pillows on the floor – what else?! Dr. Watanabe, who I refer to as Bobby, asked me if I wanted to go to Japan. I was delightfully startled by this question. It actually blew me away with a huge sense of excitement, and I said to Bobby, "Do I ever want to go to Japan!!" I wanted to see where Bobby's parents had come from. Bob was a Nisei, which means second generation of Japanese. How Bobby's parents, his sisters and himself had come to spend about four years in a camp where American Japanese were taken and locked up, and how Bob and I had met, is another story.

Now that I had made it known so clearly, to all that were at that dinner, that I wanted to be on my way to Japan, Bob decided that a man named George Yasinaga, who had gone to high school with Bob, probably at that camp where they were forced to reside, was to start teaching me Japanese immediately. Actually Bob had to learn the language too, since he was an American boy. He could understand what his dad was saying to him but in response Bob could only say "OK".

I must now say that George Yasinaga and I got along like oil and water! Bob wanted George, at George's request, to escort me all the way to and from Japan to act as my interpreter, but I didn't want any part of that scenario. After a few days of internal debate between the three of us, I won and I was on my way alone to Japan. My mission was to try to get a Japanese distributor for two of our films that my then husband Anthony Cardoza and I had produced, and Bob had kindly invested in. Also, however, I wanted to interest the Japanese in auto racing – namely, my auto racing. I had at that point been in two Demolition Derbies, one of which was on the Wide World of Sports, and the other in the Cow Palace in San Francisco.

I climbed onto the airplane at LAX that would take me to Hawaii, and from there I would transfer to Air Siam. One of Bob's other friends owned a travel agency, and he booked me to travel, along with some tour group. I was told that when I reached Tokyo I should just lose myself from the people on the tour. The plan was that I would be picked up by one of Bob's friends, who was the manager of the Pacific Hotel. Thank goodness my name was on my jumpsuit so that I could be claimed by the unknown person who had been sent to pick me up. I was having problems getting through customs, and I didn't know why this customs agent was so upset with me. A Japanese student who was on my fight came to my rescue! It seems that the custom agent wanted me to print on the form that had been handed to me on the plane just before we landed in Japan, and the way I had written out the information was impossible for this agent to read.

Little did I know, at the time, what was in store for me. This was the exact time that our Marine fighter pilots had just been ordered out of Vietnam and had landed in the far tip of Japan. On the first early morning of my stay in Japan, the phone rang in my room at the Pacific Hotel. It was a man named Jimmy Fukuzaki, who was, at that time, in charge of the USO in

Japan. Now Frank Sinatra had a secretary who was a dear friend of mine, and I had called her to tell her that I was going to Japan. Frank Sinatra's secretary had let Jimmy Fukuzaki in Japan know that I was coming, and this was how he knew how to get in touch with me. Jimmy Fukuzaki called and asked if I would be available to take a trip the next morning to pay a visit to my Marine friends. Of course I said yes, thinking I would *be driving a few miles down the road.* Now all I knew about the Marines at that time was that they fought on the ground. I was naïve. I didn't know that there were Marine Pilots, as well. I was picked up at a Military Airport outside Tokyo and escorted onto a c-type plane that I had flown in Vietnam with Dale Robertson. We flew for six hours to the tip of Japan. During the flight I heard these American pilots trying to understand what the Japanese on the radio were saying to them. You see, in 1975 our American military and the Japanese civilians just didn't understand each other's language. It was a great wonder that we made it safely to our destination, always wondering if we were actually going in the right direction. The plan was for me to stay the night at the Marine Base. I had taken my auto racing film with me to show at the officer's club to my newfound friends. Well, did I feel silly when I got off that plane and looked up into the sky at these enormous fighter jets!!

55

I thought my auto racing films and what I did in a racecar were just plain dumb next to what these men had flown and the job that they had been required to do. Once again my military friends tried to pump up my confidence by saying they didn't know how to ride a motorcycle. You see, I was wearing one of my Bates leathers outfits, trimmed with a fringe, that I wore while riding a motorcycle in parades. Yes, I was very adept at riding motorcycles and racing cars, but certainly not in flying a fighter jet. Now trying to make me feel more at home in the athletic sphere, it was suggested to me in the Officer's Club that one of the pilots could fly me out to sea and I could parachute out. I immediately embraced this idea and I eagerly agreed, but when the Commanding Officer got wind of it, the adventure was nixed. The evening ended with my showing my auto racing films to a very polite group of Marine pilots, who were desperately missing their families. The next morning I was flown back to Tokyo to continue on with my own personal mission.

I learned a great deal about the way the Japanese lived in Tokyo, but that is another story. The Harlem Globe trotters, who were also staying at the hotel, referred to me, as Annie Oakley, because of the way I dressed.

That was the end of our military presence in Vietnam, and now what I do is visit our traveling Vietnam Wall, wherever it might be. My garage is still filled with letters and mementoes from my military pen pals during the

ten years when I was known as Joy Wilkerson, "Miss South Vietnam".

The rest of my adventurous trip to Japan I have documented in letters

that I sent home. It seems I was hungry most of the time, having run out of

funds. As a guest of the USA military I had always been cared for.

Sincerely

JOY WILKERSON

Joy Wilkerson

Joy Wilkerson wearing her hair rollers in Vietnam April of 1967. Joy was visiting her GI friends on her one day off in the bush country of Vietnam. After Joy's Green Beret escort got Joy out of there via a helicopter two of Joy's friends were killed one of which was also beheaded. Joy's military friends said that they loved seeing her hair rollers as it reminded them of home.

Joy Wilkerson on stage Vietnam April, 1967

Eakin Compound Cantho

Joy Wilkerson on stage in Vietnam April, 1967

On Joy Tour of Vietnam on USS Teconderoga

Joy washed her hair in the early dawn

About the Author:

Joy Wilkerson was named as one of the **"Two Thousand Women of Achievement** 1971". She was one of the few women to start in the racing businesses. Her show biz career started from 1962 , with five Danny Thomas Specials on Television, She was the entertainer for many charities, such as: Blind Children's Foundation, Multiple Sclerosis, March of Dimes, and mainly the U.S.O. She was awarded the title of: Miss South Vietnam given by all the U.S.A. Military Services, for USO work and after trip to Vietnam with Dale Robertson in 1967. Over the course of her career, she has received numerous awards and recognition's for her charitable work given by various branches of military services, and certificate of achievement from many other charities.

Wilkerson also appeared on hundreds of T.V. and radio talk shows around the world. She also co-starred in: "Bigfoot" with John Carradine and Lindsay Crosby. Her other film credits are: "Run Angel Run"(girlfriend to William Smith) and "They Only Kill Their Masters", starring James Garner. She's also a lecturer, broadcaster and TV hostess of "The Joy Wilkerson Show" written, produced and directed by motion picture film-maker, Anthony Cardoza. The half hour variety/talk show was syndicated in the U.S.and sold internationally

The energetic Ms. Wilkerson dabbled in a variety of sports, including auto racing, in which the famous racing promoter gave her her first try in an all women stock car race at Ascot Park Speedway, in Gardena, California. Prior to her fender banging experience, she was a trophy girl at that track and fell in love with the speeding sprint and midget race cars on the half mile clay oval, where she presented the winning hardware to famous speedsters, in her shocking pink micro-mini dresses.

Wilkerson also raced against astronaut legend Pete Conrad in a Toyota-match race at Watkins Glen.. New York. She also competed in ABC-N's "Wide World Of Sports"

Demolition Derby against Cha'Cha' Muldowney, the drag racing queen and Ricky Nelson, Pernelli Jones and a host of other Indianapolis drivers.

Some of the cars she drove were TQ midgets, full sized midgets, sprint cars, dune buggies, SCCA-Formula Fords at Willow Springs, Stock Cars at 605 Speedway. She drove at Flemington Speedway (N.J.) and paced the NASCAR hotshoes at Ontario Motor Speedway, in a Datsun 280-Z for the Winston-500 mile stock car race. She also drove Gary Bettenhausen's sprint car in Terre Haute, Indiana. Not claiming to be a champion race driver, she did it to help the future ladies in motor racing get publicity and notoriety. In one case. She met an astronaut's/Indy 500 racer and taught her how to get

PR for herself. The lady driver went on to make a name for herself in the racing history books.

Wilkerson's other attributes are ballroom dancing, swimming, horseback riding, jogging, skipping rope, public relations, skating and FAST CARS.

Danny Thomas (a second cousin) started Wilkerson's career in showbiz and Bob Hope sent her to her first trophy-girl presentation to Riverside international Raceway (California) which unknowingly connected her with the auto racing world. Born a Leo, she fits right into the limelight of Hollywood and the kleiglights that brightens her being who she is. JOY WILKERSON.

Printed in the United States
24573LVS00001B/52-150

9 781410 740052